THE MANNERS PLAY BOOK

THE MANNERS PLAYBOOK

Essential Lessons for Young
African-American Boys on Self-Awareness,
Confidence and Etiquette

JAMES B. WINGO, M.Ed.

publish your gift

THE MANNERS PLAYBOOK

Copyright © 2021 James B. Wingo, M.Ed.

All rights reserved.

Published by Publish Your Gift®
An imprint of Purposely Created Publishing Group, LLC

No part of this book may be reproduced, distributed or transmitted in any form by any means, graphic, electronic, or mechanical, including photocopy, recording, taping, or by any information storage or retrieval system, without permission in writing from the publisher, except in the case of reprints in the context of reviews, quotes, or references.

Contact Amber N. Ford at ambernford.com

Contact Corine Adams-Bell at houseofcree@gmail.com

Contact James Wingo at
IG: @global_ecs | FB: GLOBAL_ECS | info@globablecs.net

Printed in the United States of America

ISBN: 978-1-64484-361-1 (print)
ISBN: 978-1-64484-362-8 (ebook)

Special discounts are available on bulk quantity purchases by book clubs, associations and special interest groups. For details email: sales@publishyourgift.com or call (888) 949-6228.
For information logon to: www.PublishYourGift.com

A MESSAGE TO THE BOYS IN MY FAMILY

To my young grandsons Sincere Dawson, Sage and Justus Metcalf, and my great-nephews Noaan Wingo, Kobe and Daniel Pitts Jr., I dedicate this book to all of you as the future of our family's legacy. I want you to always remember that you have the spirit of past Kings in our family and race. Let no one tell you that you have no culture, courage or pride. You were born to be great. It is okay for you to have your style, but have manners, etiquette and humility. I love you and cannot wait to see what great success you are about to have.

Love always,
Papa Wingo

TABLE OF CONTENTS

Acknowledgments 1

WHAT IS ETIQUETTE? 3
   What Is Etiquette? Exercise 9

PUBLIC ETIQUETTE 11
   Public Etiquette Exercise 15

NEIGHBORLY ETIQUETTE 17
   Neighborly Etiquette Exercise 19

HEALTH ETIQUETTE 21
   Health Etiquette Exercise 30

DRESSING WITH ETIQUETTE 31
   Dressing with Etiquette Exercise 39

HOME ETIQUETTE 41
   Home Etiquette Exercise 43

TABLE ETIQUETTE 45
   Table Etiquette Exercise 48

RESTAURANT ETIQUETTE 53
Restaurant Etiquette Exercise 57

CONVERSATION ETIQUETTE 59
Conversation Etiquette Exercise 61

GUEST ETIQUETTE 63
Guest Etiquette Exercise 65

FRIENDSHIP ETIQUETTE 67
Friendship Etiquette Exercise 69

SOCIAL MEDIA ETIQUETTE 71
Social Media Etiquette Exercise 76

TEACHER ETIQUETTE 77
Teacher Etiquette Exercise 79

TRAVEL ETIQUETTE 81
Travel Etiquette Exercise 87

ADULTS AND ETIQUETTE 89
Adults and Etiquette Exercise 92

ETIQUETTE AND GRATITUDE 93
Etiquette and Gratitude Exercise 95

SALUTATION ETIQUETTE 97
Salutation Etiquette Exercise 99

SPORTS AND ETIQUETTE 101
   Sports and Etiquette Exercise 103

HUMBLE ETIQUETTE 105
   Humble Etiquette Exercise 107

ETIQUETTE AND BULLYING 109
   Etiquette and Bullying Exercise 114

ETIQUETTE AND LGBTQ 117
   Etiquette and LGBTQ Exercise 119

ETIQUETTE AND BODY IMAGE 121
   Etiquette and Body Image Exercise 125

SEX AND ETIQUETTE 127
   Sex and Etiquette Exercise 129

Etiquette Exercise Answers 131

About the Author 145

ACKNOWLEDGMENTS

I give my utmost respect and thankfulness to my brother, Anthony L. Wingo. You made this project look as professional as I imagined. Your expertise, ideas and vision kept my creative juices flowing. Peace and love to you always, Bruh.

Much gratitude to my grandson, Gyasi Wingo, for your vision on arrangement and picture selection. I know you will continue to be the best graphic designer out there.

Thank you to Amber N. Ford for the photographs, including my author's picture. Best of luck.

I also would like to thank Ms. Corine Adams-Bell for her added creativity in designing all of the images in my book; much appreciated, Corine.

Thank you to Dr. Mia Flowers and Dr. Gary Carrington for your expertise on the psychology of children and families. Your guidance will always be appreciated.

Thank you to my sister, Karen Wingo, who told me to think BIG and to know that I can do this. I got you, Sis!

Thank you to my sons, Skye Wingo and Kelly Wingo Dawson, and my nephews, Damon Wingo, Kern Peale Jr., Deion Sanders and Izaiah Sanders, with whom I practiced all of these techniques and ideas throughout their adolescent lives. Love you all.

Thank you to the rest of my family who gave me encouragement along the way to see the completion of this book through. I love you all.

WHAT IS ETIQUETTE?

Definition

Some will say having manners is the act of acting politely at all times; others will say it is how one acts in his culture for various reasons. Both are correct. Etiquette is how you behave with rules according to how you were reared in your culture.

In looking at this definition, many will think that there is one culture, race or ethnicity that owns the perception of what etiquette or manners look like. I am here to tell you no one race can claim that distinction. You, young man, have what it takes to learn, succeed and be accomplished. If you haven't attended a banquet or had dinner in an upscale restaurant, you are still equipped to participate. Not too long ago, Blacks weren't allowed in particular restaurants, clubs and business organizations.

We felt that we were not wanted, so why learn the customs of that establishment? You should learn those customs so you will be accepted, wherever you will travel.

This book is for men and boys of all ages, from young boys entering middle school to young men entering college. Since we were all raised differently, we may know about the basics of hygiene, or we may not. This book is for fathers, to help them navigate this information for their sons or the young boys in their lives. Likewise, this is for the mother who needs information to talk to her son about the basics of manners for men. Often, mothers feel the need to talk to their sons. Now they have a book that can help in this process. All parents want to encourage their sons to be great and be accepted for who they are—Kings!

Origin

Where do you think manners originated? Would you believe Egypt? Egypt is the birthplace of civilization. Most known facts, discoveries and societal rules were first written in Egypt, and so were manners. The first written scroll of manners was called *The Instructions of Ptahhotep*. This text was written to teach the youth how to live.

Pharaoh Djedkare Isesi, the ruler at that time, commanded that the only way you could gain knowledge was to hear it from someone who had experience. This was the vizier, the minister or highest official to advise the pharaoh, who was also his eldest son, Ptahhotep.

Historical Facts

The main themes in *The Instructions of Ptahhotep* are silence, timing, truthfulness, relationships, and *MANNERS!* So you see, we are descendants from Kings and Pharaohs and we should honor the fact that manners are not just for them but also us. The Egyptians wanted the teachings of their youth to be handed down from experienced men. Continue this legacy, young men, so our generation can benefit from your learning these skills and rules.

These etiquette rules were written on scrolls, which were found in 1847 during an excavation by an Egyptologist in Egypt. The scrolls are now housed in the National Library in Paris, France.

Speaking of France, there lived a king in France named King Henry VIII. He was a very rich and famous king. In modern terms, he might be what we call a "playa, playa." He had parties galore where he invited other rich patrons from around his town. They partied, drank, had women, food, and music and enjoyed life.

One day the gardener noticed how the king's possessions, such as his castle, his flowers and garden, even his own living spaces, weren't being respected by his rich subjects. So the king ordered the gardener to write particular rules in which *EVERYONE* must obey! He wrote signs such as "stay on the path," "stay off the roses," "no loud talking," and "no garbage throwing." He also had rules for eating, such as no eating with hands and no sharing of goblets. These were the first rules of etiquette. In fact, the French meaning of etiquette is *little sign* or *ticket*. Etiquette is simply little signs that can help guide you along the way to being hospitable.

There are plenty of rules to learn as a young man to use as you travel away from home. Even when going to a friend's house, you will learn that they may do some things that are not as familiar. Your friend's family may do things differently. The family may sit at the dinner table and eat together and have conversations. You may be used to everyone getting a plate and fork and moving to a place that's comfortable to eat. You may as well get used to conforming to different rules once you enter that new world.

This book will give you tips and rules on how to adjust and be comfortable in various settings. I will discuss many topics and things that you should know, and hopefully you use them, at least while in the company of other people. Let's have fun as we build your playbook with some good advice.

WHAT IS ETIQUETTE? EXERCISE

Select an answer for the questions below:

1. Where is the birthplace of manners?

    a) America

    b) Ethiopia

    c) Rome

    d) Egypt

2. What are manners?

    a) politeness

    b) cultural behavior

    c) lack of rudeness

    d) acting white

3. Finish the following sentences:

    Rules of etiquette came from _____. _____ is how you behave according to the rules that you were reared with in your culture. Etiquette is _____ that can help guide you along the way to being

_____. *The Instructions of Ptahhotep* was written to _____
_____.

PUBLIC ETIQUETTE

Public spaces and amenities are for everyone and therefore should be treated as such for everyone to share. You should use manners in these public spaces:

- public transportation
- parks
- pools
- museums
- movie theaters
- malls
- sidewalks and streets

A rule of thumb is to act politely. Here are some simple tips on behaving in public:

Everyone wants to have a good time at the movies. Oftentimes, we enjoy talking to the movie screen as if we are one of the actors. We get so caught up in the storyline that we tell the characters to be aware of the monster in the closet. You know that person who shouts out, "Don't open the door, NOOOOOOOO!" It can be very irritating to hear comments throughout the movie. You have to keep your emotions in check to avoid disturbing everyone around you because you are not at home! Most of all, arrive on time! It is disrespectful to cross over others while you are trying to get to your seat in the middle of the row. If you do have to cross over people to get to your seat, face them as you pass by and do not have your butt sliding past their faces. No one wants that.

Many people benefit from using public transportation. It is not a personal vehicle. Speak in a quiet tone. Be mindful of others who might have had a bad day at work or school and need to reflect on their day prior to getting home. You may be with your friends, but maintain a low tone and resist being unruly to other passengers. Give up your seat to elderly passengers and women, especially pregnant women; this would truly show you have some manners. Playing loud music is usually a no-no on public transportation. Keep earbuds in or headphones on while listening to music or watching videos. Everyone else does not have to agree with your musical taste.

Malls used to be a gathering place for young people to hang out, but now, more people are shopping online. If there is still a mall that you frequent, use manners while gathering with your friends. Be mindful of people around you—there may be elderly shoppers trying to navigate, mothers with baby strollers or walking their toddlers, or people with disabilities utilizing the space. Refrain from being animated or loud. It is nice to have fun, but it is also fun to be nice.

You might think this takes the fun away from everything that young people do. No! As previously mentioned, public places are for everyone to enjoy and should be enjoyed accordingly. What if there were a bunch of adults playing their music loud, taking up all of the seating, spreading their belongings all around? You would not be able to enjoy yourself! The point is to have fun but be mindful of people. Talk and laugh only loud enough for your private communications.

Clean up after yourself. Other people don't want to pick up your trash in order to have a clean space around them.

Stay to the right when people are approaching you. No one should have to move out of your way to walk down the street.

Stay to the side to have your conversations. Don't stop and chat with your friends where it blocks the path of anyone who wishes to get by.

PUBLIC ETIQUETTE EXERCISE

Select T for True or F for False:

1. T/F – Public places are only for young people to enjoy.

2. T/F – You have to keep your emotions in check while shopping in public places.

3. T/F – It is nice to have fun, but it is also fun to be nice.

4. T/F – Stay to the right when people are approaching you.

5. T/F – Try to talk in a loud voice so other passengers can hear you.

NEIGHBORLY ETIQUETTE

Have you officially met your neighbors? Do you speak to them if given the chance? Whether you live in a house, apartment or gated community, neighbors can be helpful, so it is a good idea to get to know who lives around you.

Regardless of where you live, there are certain etiquette rules you are expected to follow to keep the peace in your community. The rules may be slightly different based on cultural differences, but here are some that you can follow: Don't drive or walk on their side of the property. A lot of neighbors take pride in the care of their lawn and property and you should respect theirs as much as you respect yours. Do not take shortcuts and walk across your neighbors' lawns because you think it is convenient. Use common pathways (sidewalks, driveways) to walk around. If your neighbors are elderly, help them sometimes by bringing their trash cans in or out, shoveling their sidewalks or raking their leaves. I am not saying you have to do it all of the time, but if you are outside doing your yard work, volunteer to do theirs.

If you are having parties at your house or in your yard or pool, let them know in advance that you are having friends over. Inform them that you will be mindful of the noise, and give them a beginning and end time. That way, you are alerting them and they are not caught off guard. Hold true to your promise about when the event will be over. The last thing you want is the police coming by to ask you to disperse or turn the music down because you are disturbing the neighborhood.

Start building your relationships with your neighbors now and who knows, you may get a great gift for your special occasions.

NEIGHBORLY ETIQUETTE EXERCISE

List three ways you can be a good neighbor.

1.

2.

3.

HEALTH ETIQUETTE

There are many factors that contribute to overall health: hygiene, nutrition, dental health, your biology, exercise and physical exams. Let us start with hygiene.

Hygiene

As a young man there's nothing more embarrassing than to be asked, "What's that smell?" Of course you will say, "What, who me? It is not me!" Then you will take a sniff and you will know it is you!

If you take a shower on Monday, you cannot assume it will last for several days. Even if you think you did not sweat, you still have to shower or bathe. If you wear your clothes for multiple days, they may look clean, but trust me—they are not. You cannot use excuses that your mom didn't wash your clothes yet. You have to start taking the responsibility of helping her wash clothes or washing your clothes by yourself. If you live in a situation where there are a lot of family members and you cannot afford to wash regularly, this may present a problem for you. The bottom line is that you cannot go around with soiled clothes and expect no one will notice. You might have to wash some clothing articles—items like underwear, socks and tee shirts—by hand with soap. You can wash them out at night and hang them up to dry by morning. I know it will be difficult, but you will have to figure it out with your parent or guardian; it has to get done. It can be rough, but as a young man, you will have to do laundry yourself. As a young man, you have to depend on yourself to do it and not someone else.

As you grow older, you may be by yourself, such as in college, the armed services or living abroad, and you will have to do it yourself. Your parent/guardian may not be there, so grow up, young man, and get started.

Body

Along with having clean clothes and underwear, you must wash your body! Showering or bathing every other day won't cut it. You must wash your body every day. There may be obstacles because of your living conditions, but you must find a way.

I once had to live in my car while I was job hunting in Atlanta. Before I went to sleep in my car at night, I would unfold the clothes I was going to wear the next day. I would lay them on the folded-down seats of the car and put other clothes on top as a mattress. In the morning, those laid out clothes on the bottom would have fewer wrinkles. I would go to a nearby gas station to wash my face, brush my teeth and put on those laid out clothes. I was now ready to look for work. Adversity can help us to find a way to be presentable and clean.

For the younger readers, washing up is particularly important because as men we have to keep those body parts clean because of our sweat, e.g., under our armpits, under and around our scrotum (balls) and penis and between our butt cheeks—yeah, you can laugh. When we perspire, the sweat exits our skin and eventually dries up if it is not wiped off. If sweat dries, this does not mean that the sweat will not smell.

For the older readers, you will want to use wet wipes after you go poop. Those brown streaks are caused by excess poop. You have to wash every day to get that excess poop from between those butt cheeks. Stop laughing, I am serious! Some of you are not wiping well enough, and if you are, it still smells eventually, so you have to shower or bathe every day. They now make wet wipes for men that are strong and do not break up easily.

If you are only taking showers, I suggest you try to take a nice, long bath at least once per month. The reason is that your body reacts differently when you soak for a while. Soaking helps the muscles to rejuvenate, especially for you athletes. It repairs the muscles, refreshes your skin and helps soak out toxins that are in your skin. Showers are great for getting in and out quickly, but a monthly bath can do wonders. That is the difference between a shower and bath. As long as you choose one of them on a daily basis, you cannot go wrong.

Skin

Your facial skin has to be washed daily to keep oil and dirt from getting deep into your pores. You can put skin moisturizer or lotion on your face to keep it fresh, clean and glowing. By not cleaning and moisturizing your skin, you will speed up the possibilities of zits, acne and the like. I am sure you don't want to start having those problems.

Hair

While you are in the shower, wash your hair. For those with longer hair or dreadlocks, you may not want to wash it every couple of days, but when you do, here are some techniques:

- Short hair: wash every day and use a hair conditioner every couple of days and also hair oil or gel afterward to keep your hair shiny and clean.

- Long hair: wash every day and use a conditioner or moisturizer to keep your hair in good condition.

- Dreadlocks: sponge wash your hair lightly so you don't untangle the dreadlocks and use a moisturizer to keep the dreadlocks shiny; oil your hair after every washing.

Hands and Feet

You might think taking care of your fingernails and toenails is unimportant since you are showering or bathing—they get clean automatically, right? No! You have to make an effort to clean your fingernails and toenails. Do not put your fingers in and around your mouth where you will inject germs and bacteria. Fingernails carry so many germs that you can get sick with diarrhea or vomiting. Scrub behind those fingernail tips to get that dirt out. If you don't have a nail brush in the house, use an old toothbrush to scrub and keep them clean.

The toenails are just as important. If you do not wash them, it could lead to toenail fungus or athlete's foot. If you are very active athletically and are in and out of showers a lot, wear a pair of slides to avoid those foot infections.

Mouth

Brushing your teeth is important. Half of the diseases you can catch start from your mouth and teeth. Think of the food you put in your mouth that gets stuck between your teeth and gums. That food will stay there *alllll* night, fermenting between your teeth and staining your teeth enamel. That fermented food begins to rot and smell, and you begin to have bad dental hygiene.

Brush at least two times per day to get rid of that excess food left in your mouth and floss out that food from in between your teeth. You will begin to have fresh breath and won't chase the other kids away. Brush and floss, dude, it will help your life tremendously!

Diet

Another concern that most young men neglect is eating properly. I am talking about the fast foods and snacks on the go. Getting a healthy diet of veggies, juices, *water* and less fried foods and less meat will help you toward a healthy body.

Try fasting for a meal or two when you know you have overindulged without working out. Consult someone on being a vegetarian or vegan; it won't hurt. Some of the strongest athletes and most talented artists are vegetarian or vegan, such as Colin Kaepernick, Kyrie Irving, RZA, Beyoncé, Mike Tyson and Stevie Wonder. These are just a few and they are doing quite well.

Physical

I mentioned working out: this is essential to the development of your body. You might ask, "what does this have to do with etiquette?" Well, a healthy body is *always* a sign of having discipline, rules and manners. Do something physical inside the house or go outside to play in your local playground, go to the gym or participate in a sport or activity at your school. You can ride your bike around the neighborhood, jog, do calisthenics or take the stairs. You can do push-ups and sit-ups before bedtime, stretch, jump rope or lift weights. Go outside and play Frisbee, roller-skate or skateboard. Stay active and do whatever it takes to work your body out. A healthy body breeds a healthy mind!

Doctor

I would like to speak about visiting your doctor on a semi-annual or annual basis. Visiting the doctor early in life can help you prevent a lot of concerns that may affect you later on. No one wants to be told by a doctor what you should have done at a younger age to prevent a particular disease or symptom. Now you have to take medications and have surgeries when it may have been prevented earlier.

A doctor can recommend how to remedy your concerns *before* they get out of hand. Doctors can warn you of certain practices and habits that you are doing that are not good for you. Doctors cannot force you to stop bad habits, but they can definitely warn you of what could happen to you if you continue those habits.

A lot of men are afraid or just stubborn about going to the doctor. Men mistakenly feel it is a waste of time. They feel they are healthy and there is nothing wrong. That is the wrong attitude. The whole point of going to the doctor is to make sure you are as healthy as you can be. A man's ego is so strong it will tell him, *keep going, you are alright!* Good advice from a doctor is always helpful, whether you want to hear it or not.

HEALTH ETIQUETTE EXERCISE

1. What are four things you can do to improve your health?

    a)

    b)

    c)

    d)

2. Drinking LESS water can improve your diet.

    True or False

3. The health of your body may not affect the health of your mind.

    True or False

4. You should see a doctor every two to three years.

    True or False

DRESSING WITH ETIQUETTE

How we dress is a true indication of who we are. Through clothing we are able to express ourselves and show our unique individuality. In being unique we must remember to take into account where we are going and what the occasion is.

For instance, if you were playing basketball you would not wear football cleats or ice skates to the gym. You would look pretty ridiculous. The same applies to going to an event; you want to fit in and not stand out if you can. Going out with our friends can be fun because we usually dress casual. Everyone will want to put on their coolest outfits to show that they have some style and can blend in with their friends. If you dress casually in sneakers, hoodies, hats and tees, that may be fine when hanging out with your friends. But what if you are invited to a birthday party at a social entertainment center or restaurant, a wedding, a banquet or a special occasion? That is when you have to up your game and dress accordingly.

If you are invited somewhere it is always good to ask, "What's the attire?" Meaning, how should I dress? Most of the time you will probably guess the attire for casual invitations such as being invited over to your friend's house for dinner with their family or their birthday party.

What if it is a bar mitzvah, an awards banquet or at a restaurant? You ask! Girls and women do it all the time; young men, you need to start asking what to wear also. The last thing you want is for everyone looking at you with big smiles on their faces because you are unprepared. Don't be the gag of the party, not if you can help it.

The younger you are, the more acceptable it is for you to be out of place. But as you get older, into your late teens, you want to be properly dressed. Every teen should have at least one dark sport coat, pair of slacks or dark suit in their wardrobe. When I say dark, I mean black, navy blue or grey. If it is a loud color like red, green or white, it will be noticeable that you are wearing that outfit again. By having at least one dark outfit, you can wear it multiple times and be accepted at any place. You also will need at least one white-collar shirt and dark tie.

Dark sneakers are not dress shoes. You may see your famous stars or celebrities dressed in sneakers and suits, but for practical purposes, until you are rich and famous, let's go with dress shoes, not sneakers. As a matter of fact, there are some establishments that will not allow sneakers, jeans and tee shirts on their premises. Having these items—dress shoes, collared shirts and a sweater or a jacket —will make sure you can follow their dress code.

What about African clothing? All African-American young men should have several outfits like a dashiki or a cultural dress of your family background, whether it is from the Caribbean or native Africa. Choosing when and where to wear it will depend on the occasion. To be safe, ask your parents or host.

Suits and Sport Coats

As you grow older, you can certainly start adding to your suit/jacket wardrobe. Items with tans and stripe patterns can give you more of a variety. Wearing attire like suits, jackets and dress shoes can boost your wardrobe. If you take good care of these items you will not have to buy them repeatedly.

As you wear attire such as suits, jackets and dress shoes, it will be economical if you learn how to care for them. Always hang your suits and jackets up once you return home. Hang your slacks on a pants hanger that's sturdy enough to hold them without bending the hanger. If the hanger bends, it will wrinkle your slacks and they will look horrible the next time you wear them.

The same goes for your sport coat. Put it on a hanger that's sturdy, not a shirt hanger, because it will make your jacket look saggy and ill fitting the next time you wear it. You can probably wear your jacket at least three to four times before it needs to be cleaned. If there are stains or wrinkles, it should be sent to the dry cleaners.

Shirts you can probably only wear once. Check the collar on the shirt; if it looks like it has a shadow, that is sweat and it will need cleaning. You can wash it yourself or send it to the dry cleaners.

Your shoes should be wiped off if there is any dust or dirt on them. If you don't have any shoe trees, then stuff your shoes with newspapers or plastic bags to keep the shape of the shoe. If you buy a quality pair of shoes, they will last you a long time—if your feet are not growing! Here are some suggestions on what to wear on various occasions. Always ask, what's everyone wearing?

Parties

Wear your best casual clothes, clean jeans, pants, a shirt (no tee shirt), sneakers and no hats unless it is outside. Don't be afraid to ask what to wear if the invitation is verbal. If you receive a written invitation, it will probably say what to wear by stating the theme of the occasion or it will list specifically what to wear.

Weddings

If you have been asked to "BE IN" the wedding you will be instructed on what to wear, usually a tuxedo or a suit. If you are not in the wedding, wear dress slacks/pants and shirt and dress shoes. You can dress it up with a jacket or vest or suit and tie.

Funerals

If it is your family, you can ask a relative what to wear, but usually it will be dark slacks/pants, white shirt and dress shoes. You can choose to wear a jacket or suit and tie. If you don't have any white shirts then wear a shirt that has a collar.

Miscellaneous

Banquets: Suit or sport coat, dress shirt, tie and dress shoes.

Celebrations: Always ask. You don't want to go casual when everyone is in dress clothes or come in dress clothes and everyone is casual.

School awards: Slacks, shirt and dress shoes, or you may be told to wear your school uniform.

Dates: If it is at the movies, then of course dress casual. If it is at a restaurant, then call to find out the dress code. If you are trying to impress, then up your game and dress it up! I am pretty sure your date will be dressing to impress you, so don't disappoint them. If they accepted your invitation, show them that you appreciate them joining you!

If you are going to wear a tie and you don't know how to tie it, then go on YouTube and search for a video on how to tie a tie. There are plenty of videos that can instruct you on how to tie a neck tie or bow tie. I learned by having someone teach me, step by step. Some of you may not have someone to show you, so YouTube will be your best friend. There are also good videos on how to shine your shoes and how to care for them, so look at some of them to get some good tips.

DRESSING WITH ETIQUETTE EXERCISE

1. When you are invited to an event, it is rude to ask what to wear.

   True or False

2. You should fold your suit/jacket and pants after you wear them so they will fit neatly in a drawer.

   True or False

3. What is proper wedding attire?

   a) clothing to match the groom

   b) casual clothes to be comfortable

   c) at least dress pants, a collared shirt and dress shoes

   d) colors that your date is wearing

HOME ETIQUETTE

You might think, "manners at home are so easy; since I live there, what could be the problem?" Well, plenty! Having manners at home is really respecting your home because more than likely, you didn't pay for it. Even if you did pay for it, you would want to keep a home that is harmonious, safe and respectable. Let's start with:

Your Room

Are you picking up after yourself as far as dirty clothes on the floor and paper wrappers from food and beverages? You are of the age where it would be a kind thing to do, to ease the workload of your parents/guardians. This is also teaching you how to live away from home. One day, you will have roommates and will want a good relationship with whom you are living with.

Are you making your bed every day? There's nothing worse than coming home and not having enough room to even relax because of sheets hanging off the side of the bed, covers on the floor and pillowcases that haven't been changed in weeks. Make up your bed. It will help organize your day and it will put you in a good mood when you return that night for a good night's sleep.

Kitchen

Are you doing your share of washing dishes or loading the dishwasher? Helping to do your share will bring smiles to your parents' faces. Don't keep piling dishes in the sink expecting someone else to do them for you. Start a habit now so when you do move out you will know what a clean kitchen should look like. If you see dishes in the sink, wash them. When you do clean the kitchen, do it completely, i.e., clean the stove, sweep the floor and wipe off the countertops! Practice makes perfect!

Living Space

When you leave the play area for the evening, make sure it looks as neat as it can: leave no excess paper wrappers on the floor, put dirty dishes in the kitchen sink and wash them, straighten the pillows and covers in the seating area and place the remote controls where the next person can find them. The worst thing in the world is when you are ready to watch the TV and you cannot find the remote.

HOME ETIQUETTE EXERCISE

1. It is only necessary to clean your room every other week.

   True or False

2. It would be better for mothers or sisters to clean rooms because they do it better.

   True or False

3. It is better to stack dishes in the sink so that the next person will have it easier in washing the dishes.

   True or False

4. It is better for the younger sibling to clean the living space so they can learn how to do it.

   True or False

TABLE ETIQUETTE

Sitting at a formal table setting for the first time can be quite daunting to say the least. At home we may be used to having a fork, knife and spoon (flatware), but to see more than three pieces of flatware we may think what do we use first and with which food items?

The first time I was at an event, it was an awards banquet. There were about ten of us sitting at a round table with flatware on our left and right, glasses to our left and right. *Which is mine, where do I start?*

The first thing I did was look around and see what everyone else was doing, and of course they were looking around just like me, lol! So here are some tips:

- Your drinking glasses will always be to your right. America is set up for people who are right-handed.

- Your flatware: a knife and spoons will be to your right and forks will be to your left.

- When the food arrives, start using flatware from the outside and move in toward your plate.

- If the fork has three tines, that's for your *hors d'oeuvres* (pronounced like oar-derves). *Hors d'oeuvres* are small, delicious appetizers that are served before your main meal.

- The middle fork is for salads; the largest fork is for your main meal.

- To your right, the largest spoon will be for your soup; the smallest is for your dessert, coffee and tea.

- The large knife is for cutting your food or opening a dinner roll if there isn't a small knife near the top of the plate or in the butter dish.

There are two main ways of holding your flatware. The first is called continental. To use the continental style, you hold the fork in your left hand with the tines sticking in your food and your index finger on the backside of the fork. You hold the knife in your right hand while cutting your food. Without putting either flatware down, use the fork to put the food into your mouth. Don't put the knife down either. Cutting another piece of food, you repeat the process. You can use your right hand with the knife to push the veggies or sauce onto the cut piece of food to put directly into your mouth again. Make sure the pieces are small enough to fit into your mouth so you are able to chew your food with your mouth closed. Putting a large piece of food into your mouth will cause food and sauce to fall into your lap or plate.

The other style of holding your flatware is called the American. The American style is where you hold the knife in your right hand, fork in your left, you cut your food the same way except when finished cutting you lay the knife on your plate, put the fork in your right hand and pick the food up with the fork and eat it. Then you transfer the fork from your right hand to your left hand and repeat the process. All of this changing back and forth can be cumbersome. I like the continental style, keeping the fork and knife in each hand.

TABLE ETIQUETTE EXERCISE

The Dinner

The Awards Banquet Dinner was pretty fancy this year, and every state college recruiter was in attendance. Your high school illustrated how proud they were of their college recruitment program for their seniors. Each table setting had a soup and salad bowl, a large plate with a smaller plate on top of it, a water glass and two sets of utensils: forks, spoons and knives. The soup was served first, followed by a salad, and then the main course—steak, potatoes and broccoli. Water was the beverage.

Choose one selection for each question below:

1. Which utensil do you use for the salad?

    a) small fork with three tines

    b) large spoon

    c) medium fork

    d) large fork

2. Which utensil do you use for the soup?

    a) big spoon

    b) butter knife

    c) small spoon

    d) small fork

    e) none, I like to slurp

3. Which utensil do you use for the main meal?

    a) all of the utensils

    b) large fork and large knife

    c) small fork and small knife

    d) only use the forks

4. Which utensil do you use for dessert?

    a) small fork

    b) large fork

    c) small spoon

    d) large spoon

5. At a table setting, your drinking glasses will be on your right___ left___.

6. You should always use the largest fork for all of the food.

    True or False

7. Soup is served right before desserts.

    True or False

8. What are two ways of holding your flatware; American and _____.

    a) European

    b) international

    c) continental

9. When using the American style, you only use one utensil.

    True or False

RESTAURANT ETIQUETTE

Eating at a restaurant can be fun and enjoyable. Socializing with friends, family or taking someone out to eat can also be very nerve-racking. First, research the restaurant you are going to dine at so you can become familiar with their policies and menu. Even if you are the one who was invited, you should Google it to see what type of atmosphere it has and what the dress requirements are. A lot of upscale restaurants may require a reservation, jacket or private invitation, so be aware.

When making a reservation, the restaurant is going to ask you how many are in the dinner party. The restaurant will let you know if your time for dinner is available. You should also ask what types of payments they accept (cash or which credit cards). You don't want to be embarrassed by pulling out a credit card and being told the restaurant doesn't accept that one. Then you will be running to find an ATM!

The first person you will meet will be a greeter or *maître d'*. They will greet you and ask if you have a reservation and if you do, they will escort you and your guest to a table.

Once seated, a waiter will come to your table, greet you again and introduce him or herself and possibly tell you what specials are being offered that are not on the menu. They will also make a suggestion as to what is a good choice to select for your meal.

The waiter will give you a menu and set the table with a glass of water, maybe a basket of bread, and ask if he can bring you anything you would like to drink while you look over the menu. While talking to you he has probably pulled out the napkins and may drape one over your female guest's lap and disappear while you are looking over the menu.

If you are not escorted to your table and the greeter states you can choose your own seating, then it would be considerate of you to ask your date where they would like to sit. After their choice, escort them to the table and pull out the chair for them.

Since you are familiar with the restaurant because you Googled it (RIGHT?), you can inform your guest of the type of food that is on the menu and what you are interested in eating. Discussing the food items on the menu is a good conversation piece to break the ice and helps make you more comfortable to talk. Once you have ordered your food, remember to try and keep the conversation mutual by listening to your date/friends and also sharing your stories. A no-no is continually looking at your phone! Pay attention to your date and friends or family, and remember the etiquette rules you learned earlier.

Once the dinner is over it is now time to pay for your meal. Look over your bill to make sure what you ordered is on the bill and to see whether the restaurant has already added the gratuity. A gratuity is a tip that you are going to pay that's added to the bill. If the gratuity is not on the bill, it is customary to tip your waiter and the waitstaff 15 to 20 percent for the service that you received. The waitstaff consists of the waiter who greeted you at the table and the busboy, who brought your food and/or cleared your table of dirty dishes. The waiter will usually check on you and your guest to see if the meals are to your liking and whether they can bring you anything. They will refill your water glass and get you flatware if you should drop them accidentally on the floor. If they took care of you in a nice and pleasant way, then leave them a good tip.

Tipping began in Europe with aristocrats in the seventeenth century. They would pay an amount, "To Insure Promptness" (TIP), to make sure they would get served quickly. It gradually moved to the Americas where rich Americans began to use the custom through the time of the Civil War.

After the Civil War during Jim Crow, racist restaurants and bar owners would use tipping to pay the freed slaves instead of giving them wages. This custom has continued to where it is legal to pay a restaurant employee $2.13 per hour and let the tips be considered as their salary. So when you see these individuals working hard to earn a living in the restaurant business, please be cognizant that a good tip will be appreciated.

Also, around 150 years ago, Blacks were hired to serve white customers on the railroad train. These men were called porters. They were underpaid and were only paid by tips. Even though there was a lot of racism and degradation from their customers, they made it possible for future generations of Black people to go to college and become members of the "Talented Tenth." *The Talented Tenth* was written by W. E. B. Du Bois. He believed that a certain amount of the Black class needed to be leaders by going to college and obtaining careers in professional occupations such as lawyer, doctor and politician.

RESTAURANT ETIQUETTE EXERCISE

1. When eating at a restaurant it is not necessary to have reservations if you are using a credit card.

   True or False

2. A *maître d'* will handle and bring your food to you.

   True or False

3. It is always good to check your phone repeatedly while at dinner in case there's an emergency.

   True or False

4. Upscale restaurants don't require a tip since they are expensive.

   True or False

5. Where did tipping begin?

   a) America

   b) after the Civil War

   c) Europe

   d) when slaves weren't being paid

CONVERSATION ETIQUETTE

Whether you have been invited to dinner by a friend, are on a date, or are attending a wedding or celebration, there are conversational rules to follow in order to have a good time:

Most of all, acknowledge your date by thanking them for the invite or for accepting your invite. Compliment them on their attire and use the menu to start a conversation. Find out what they're about, their goals and aspirations in life. Do they see themselves being an entrepreneur, going to college, working on community solutions? What is it that makes them tick?

Try not to focus on you the whole conversation. You can focus on your likes and dislikes too, but don't dwell on yourself the entire conversation. You are there to get to know your date better—their questions will come in time when they want to know about you.

If you are at an awards program or an interview for a college or a job, you will want to focus more on your goals and aspirations. This is an opportunity to learn more about the person or company that is meeting you. Do your homework before going to the event by learning everything you can about them. How often do they promote in their company? Do they get offers from professional teams on recruitments or drafts? You don't want to sit there talking about your personal life unless they ask you.

Focus on the purpose of the meeting, not the food. The meal will be a distraction to see how you are socially, if you have manners, if you eat with one utensil, if you talk with your mouth full of food. My future Kings, did you know that you pass food to the left and you ask food to be passed to you? You should say thank you, please and you are welcome.

Speak slowly and look your company in the eye when you do speak. You may think this should be normal but you'd be surprised at the nervousness you may experience; it can keep you off your game by forgetting to do the simple things. Relax, take your time and you will be great.

CONVERSATION ETIQUETTE EXERCISE

1. It is always good to just talk about you so that your date can get to know you better.

   True or False

2. When is the best time to learn about a company or college?

   a) after you meet them to see if they lied

   b) before you meet them so you can ask questions

   c) once you get to the school or job

   d) none of the above

GUEST ETIQUETTE

Being invited into someone's home can be an indication that they like and trust you. Be appreciative of that invitation to their home. Take a little gift of appreciation when you arrive to show your gratitude. Always say please, thank you and excuse me. When offered a drink, ask for water first unless they insist on you having juice or soda.

Do not go into their refrigerator without their permission. Do not drink all of the soda. Do not take the last of whatever snacks they give you. Pick up behind yourself and leave the bathroom clean after you have used it. Respect their property by keeping your feet on the floor and not on the sofa or chairs—even if you see their family is doing it.

Remember, they may have customs that you don't do at your home, so be cautious of how you act. For instance, they may eat at the dinner table all together as a family or they may eat in various rooms—you will have to adjust and enjoy.

If you are invited over for a "Bearthday" party or celebration you should always take a gift. Present it to the guest of honor and wait to be escorted to where the party is. I use the word "Bearthday" in place of "Birthday" to signify your born day on Earth. It's just a different use of terminology that you may not have heard before. If you are thirteen years old, some might say you have traveled around the sun thirteen times. These are just certain expressions used in the Black community.

If you are meeting your date's parents for the first time, it would be mannerable to take a small bouquet of flowers for the mom.

When leaving an event, always let the host or parent know that you enjoyed yourself and it was a pleasure to meet them.

GUEST ETIQUETTE EXERCISE

1. Being a guest in someone's home, you should:

    a) wear your best clothes to impress

    b) bring a small gift of appreciation

    c) bring your own food

    d) none of the above

2. You should behave the same as your friends in their home.

    True or False

3. Since the parents will be busy, always thank them after you get home.

    True or False

4. For a Bearthday party, it is not necessary to bring a gift if you are their friend.

    True or False

FRIENDSHIP ETIQUETTE

The key to making good friends is establishing a good relationship. Be as honest as you can and have the courage to monitor your communication when it is not hurtful. In your conversation, try using words such as thank you; I am sorry; excuse me; that was really awesome what you just did; and good job! How you talk to someone can really go a long way. In fact, being truthful will go just as well especially if the person is looking for the truth.

One dilemma that can destroy a friendship is gossip. If someone brings you information on one of your friends or someone you know, you must think about why they came to you to give you this information. Do not pass this information on. First, you don't know if it is true, and second, they may deny that they said it. Always change the subject when someone does bring you gossip and keep it positive moving forward. If it is from your friend, you have to be careful with sharing this information unless they tell you it is okay.

Protecting one's privacy is a key factor in keeping friends. If your friend is trusting to share information about them, I am sure they don't want you going around sharing it with other people. Secrecy may be hard but it is not as bad as losing a friend all because you couldn't keep a secret.

FRIENDSHIP ETIQUETTE EXERCISE

1. Two things needed to make a good friend are_____ and _____.

    a) agreement; being happy

    b) being right; agreeing more often

    c) being as honest as you can; monitoring your communication

    d) choosing one; being happy

2. Always pass the gossip to your friend so they can know how to handle it.

    True or False

3. It is good not to dwell on gossip about your friends to help them out.

    True or False

4. Text only so that you can see how they really are.

    True or False

5. Don't wait for the other person to introduce themselves.

   True or False

6. Ask as many questions as you can to find out more about them.

   True or False

7. Don't force a conversation because they are probably shy.

   True or False

SOCIAL MEDIA ETIQUETTE

In this day and age, social media is changing so quickly. The rules for using technology devices and the platforms that occupy them have have been around since only a little before you were born, and will continue changing rapidly. Your generation has grown up utilizing social media for everything: finding friends, meeting up and staying connected to friends, sharing videos and the like.

One simple rule: don't say something online that you wouldn't say in person. If you wouldn't want your family or friends to see it, then *don't hit send*. Once you hit send, you cannot get it back; it is out there in the cloud.

Don't use social media to get back at someone. It is best to say how you feel in person. You need to see peoples' body language and they need to see yours. You have to learn to communicate and listen. Nowadays you have to do both face-to-face and through text (social media).

Don't let social media be your life; use social media to help plan your life.

There have been many cases where people were bullied and they did terrible harm to themselves. This resulted from people putting terrible things on social media or the internet. Some states have laws to protect those who have been bullied and even allow people to be sued for damages.

Sexting is now illegal for those under eighteen years of age and has to be consensual between adults. You might be able to delete it, but there is a chance that someone has saved it or sent it to someone else to see. Here are some tips about cyberbullying and sexting:

- Hurtful posts can be categorized as "cyberbullying." Cyberbullying is when a person harasses another person by using hurtful words or images electronically.

- Do not send sexual pictures of someone on the internet or through social media if you are under eighteen years of age. Further, don't send pictures that you wouldn't want the world, parents or adults to see. A simple rule is to not text private body parts of each other; you never know if someone will share this information without your knowledge—how embarrassing would that be?

- Texting your girlfriend is a different story altogether. First of all, there's a lot of pressure on having a girlfriend. Do you have time for one? Are you having a girlfriend just because there's pressure to have a girlfriend? Is she pushing you to be her boyfriend? It has been proven that teens who are single have less pressure, better grades and more fun than teens who are in relationships. It is okay to say you are not ready to have a girlfriend yet.

Technology has opened up a new world of communicating to . . . THE WHOLE WORLD! Just imagine, we can keep in touch with family from near and far. It is so wonderful to chat with family members at the same time as if we are all together at home. We cannot let that bad tweet or post disrupt our harmony and togetherness.

A simple rule is: if it is not going to help the situation, don't say it! People will get the hint that something is wrong when no one is responding or commenting on a particular subject that something is wrong. Hopefully this will change their attitude on the subject and they won't speak so negatively. Once you've hurt someone's feelings with something you've said, it is very difficult to get their trust back. I'm telling you it is not worth it. Here are some more tips:

- Keep your phone on silent or off while at a public function, family event, private parties or dates. It is impolite to pay attention to your phone and not your date or invited guests.

- Before hitting send, read your message again and ask yourself: Am I hurting someone's feelings? Is it worth it? Will my parents approve of this message?

- If you are not helping the problem, don't send it.

- Remember, colleges, employers and potential friends may look at your posts to see if you are worthy of their acceptance of you.

- Try to set some boundaries on texting, posting pictures or communicating on school nights. Time can go by quickly before you realize it is one or two o'clock in the morning and you still didn't complete your homework assignment.

SOCIAL MEDIA ETIQUETTE EXERCISE

1. It is best to tell someone off on social media instead of in person—that way, they can get over it better.

   True or False

2. It is best to send your first thoughts on social media because it is the truth.

   True or False

3. If you are under the age of eighteen and your partner approves, it is okay to use sexting.

   True or False

4. Before you hit send, call your friends to warn them.

   True or False

5. Teens who have a girlfriend have more fun than those who don't.

   True or False

TEACHER ETIQUETTE

You cannot imagine how much influence your teachers have on your education. They are teaching you a subject they have mastered and studied, but they may be the one who gives you that extra credit to give you a passing grade. Your teacher might write a recommendation letter for college or recommend you for a scholarship or an internship. So why would you be rude when it is not going to make things better for you?

If you are that classroom jokester, you should curb some of those jokes for later on with your friends. I personally enjoy students in my class who have that great sense of humor, but it can be very annoying if it continues when you ask them to stop and it disrupts the class. Sometimes the jokes are to get back at the teacher because of a grade the teacher gave them or because the teacher didn't choose the student for a question or a project. Either way, it is difficult sometimes to be nice to someone you don't particularly like, but you are there for a reason and that's to get the most out of your class that you can.

You are not in class for your teacher to like you; this should not be a primary concern of yours. Your job is to learn as much as you can by being attentive and engaging. Being the class clown can cause distractions for other class members and your teacher. You never know if you might meet a teacher later on in life and be completely embarrassed by the way you acted back in school.

TEACHER ETIQUETTE EXERCISE

1. Telling good jokes in class will help calm the disruptive students.

   True or False

2. Teachers are required to give you good recommendations for college and/or jobs.

   True or False

TRAVEL ETIQUETTE

Opportunity

To have the opportunity to travel is a blessing in itself. To experience new people, places, culture and sights is beyond belief. Don't squander that opportunity. A new world can open your eyes to new options, a new way of thinking and living. When I worked for the Boys Choir of Harlem, people were always amazed by the good behavior of our boys. Did they expect us to be rowdy, rude and untrained? Well, they did.

Perception

People's perception of Black boys can be a stereotypical portrayal in the news media. The perception can be that Black boys are in gangs, have no manners, are loud and do not dress properly. We are descendants of Kings and

Queens; we wrote the book on manners in *The Instructions of Ptahhotep,* remember?

Pride

At the Boys Choir of Harlem we researched our places of travel, especially if it was out of the country. What should we expect in this new country and what will we see that will pique our interest? The boys talked later about how some of the people we saw were rude, ill-mannered and seemed like they enjoyed us more than we enjoyed them.

When traveling, you want to represent your family name and community; carry it with pride and distinction. Are your clothes cleaned and pressed? Have you packed so that you don't need help with your luggage, meaning one suitcase and one carry-on bag that can go under your seat or in an overhead bin? Do you have a small bag for all of your electronics, cords, chargers, etc.? If you are traveling by yourself or in a group, you are going to be responsible for all of your belongings. Be thoughtful because everyone cannot help you with your bags!

You will want to have a small toiletry bag that can fit:

- deodorant
- a toothbrush and travel-size toothpaste
- dental floss
- a comb/brush and hair oil
- body and face lotion for that ash in the morning after the shower
- a razor set if you are shaving
- a small bottle of cologne or body oil
- a small amount of q-tips
- a travel-size bottle of mouthwash

These items should all fit in your toiletry bag.

DON'T try to bring any weed with you. As of 2021 it is still illegal to transport marijuana across federal property and from state to state. You don't want to chance it. You will be totally embarrassed from being arrested and having to explain it to your receiving party of friends or family back home. It is not worth it!

If you are flying on an airplane for the first time, bring some gum to chew because your ears may start ringing because of the air pressure. If not, you will have to swallow often or hold your nose and breathe lightly.

If you are nervous, it's okay to let partner know that it is your first flight. They may be able to talk you through it by explaining all of the noises so you won't be nervous. Be brave but also don't feel bad if you have to let someone know that you are a little nervous. You will feel better instead of holding it in and freaking out later and being totally embarrassed.

Pay attention to the flight attendants—they are there to help you and explain what you can and cannot do. You cannot go to the restroom unless the light above your head indicates you can get up. If there is a problem and you are not sure, there's a button overhead where you can press and a flight attendant will come to you. Don't press it because you want more snacks, lol!

Walking through the airport, you want to stay to the right at all times, especially if you are on a moving walkway or on the stairs because people will want to pass on the left.

Keep your luggage and travel items with you at all times; it is your responsibility to watch them, not other strangers' unless you've had a good conversation with someone and you feel you can trust them—but to be safe, take it with you. If you are going to the restroom, most toilet stalls are big enough for a luggage bag, and your carry-on bag can hang on the back of the bathroom door.

Try to carry a few items in your wallet such as one to two credit or bank cards, a picture ID, membership card and cash. Keep your ID in your pocket along with your ticket until you get on board. You will have to show your ID at the ticket counter and at TSA (airport security) along with your ticket. Once seated you can put it back in your wallet.

Packing your suitcase will be different depending on the number of days you are going to be gone. A rule of thumb is one set of underwear for each day you are gone, plus one. You can wear jeans more than one day unless you are going to be doing some dirty activities. Bring at least one top or shirt for each day. Checking the weather before you leave will give you a good indication of what to wear: warm weather clothes or clothes for the cold, rain, and snow.

TRAVEL ETIQUETTE EXERCISE

1. How many pieces of luggage should you travel with?

    a) one per week of stay

    b) one suitcase, one carry-on bag

    c) one very large suitcase

2. When traveling by air, it is important to:

    a) use the center seat for your personal items before anyone sits there.

    b) ask for the window seat because you are a kid and they'll understand.

    c) go to the restroom before, during and after the flight.

    d) bring chewing gum because your ears may ring.

3. Always pack double clothing items for the trip in case of emergencies.

    True or False

4. Always ask someone to watch your items while you go to the restroom.

   True or False

ADULTS AND ETIQUETTE

Dealing with adults can be trying at times because they may want to do all the talking, tell you what you are doing wrong and not accept any excuses that you may offer for your situation. However, it is always wise to at least listen. Adults do have experience and knowledge that you may not know about. Adults may have experienced the same situation you are in and don't want you to repeat the same mistakes as they made in their youth.

Listening shows you have manners and respect and you will take an adult's advice into consideration. Times have changed and sometimes adults have to be brought up to speed in what is different today. Having courtesy to listen shows that you have manners.

After listening, you can offer your opinion. I hope that the adult will reciprocate the same courtesy to you. If not, then I apologize for them! I myself like to listen to young adults and really find out what's on their mind and realize maybe it is me who needs to make an adjustment.

After listening to another person's advice with undivided attention, it doesn't mean that you have to take the advice but that you will consider it in your final decision. Now if it is from your parents, you will have to change that decision rather quickly. If you've been a good communicator with your parents you may be able to explain your side and negotiate a better decision.

Not until you are on your own and paying your own bills can you disregard your parents' advice. Even then they still may know what is best for you. Living on your own will be new, so consider their advice to make your decisions. It would be foolish to disregard their advice just to show you're on your own and you feel you know it all.

You probably want to show adults close to you that you are able to handle your business and make decisions. Having more options provided to you to think about can help you in the long run. There may be something you totally forgot about or didn't know.

Growing up, you will need mentors to listen to for advice and support. It would be gracious to say, *thank you for that view of the situation and I'll have to think about my situation a bit more.* Or, *I appreciate your help and I'll have to rethink my options and possibly make a better decision.* At least you are considering their advice and can compare it to your information.

When greeting adults, it is very courteous to say "hello sir/ma'am", with a firm handshake, and it is nice to meet you. If the adult is trying to give you advice and is agreeable to you, say, "thank you very much for sharing that, I wasn't aware of it". Watching your tone of language in the presence of adults can be boring as heck, especially when you are having fun with your friends. Having good manners is always being aware of where you are and what your surroundings are about.

ADULTS AND ETIQUETTE EXERCISE

1. You should never ask adults for advice because they will just try to change your mind.

   True or False

2. Listening to adults shows:

   a) you are bored

   b) you have manners

   c) you want them to finish as soon as possible

   d) all of the above

3. You should never consider their advice because they won't think you are ready.

   True or False

4. You should thank them for their advice but let them know you are going to make your decision anyway.

   True or False

5. After introducing yourself, you should always leave quickly because you are a kid and shouldn't be around to annoy them.

   True or False

ETIQUETTE AND GRATITUDE

Show appreciation when someone does something special for you. It shows you have good manners. Don't think because you said "thank you" verbally at the time that it was sufficient. Sending the person a thank you card is more appropriate. When I say special, I mean a gift that someone gave you, your friend's parents take you out to a special dinner, an invited sleepover or a Bearthday gift.

If you are invited over for dinner, then it is okay to tell them you've enjoyed yourself very much and thank them for inviting you.

There are generic thank you cards at your stationary or drug stores where you can write your own thank you statement. If it is a blank note card, address what you are thanking them for and how you felt about them being generous and thoughtful to you. A thank you card is not necessary if they bought you a sandwich or paid your way to the movies. A simple thank you would be sufficient.

Birthday gifts, Christmas gifts, graduation gifts, invitations to a special occasion, sleepovers, or out-of-town trips all deserve a thank you card.

ETIQUETTE AND GRATITUDE EXERCISE

1. Always say thank you for any scenario and you won't have to send cards.

   True or False

SALUTATION ETIQUETTE

Meeting new people can be very scary at times. Don't worry, more than half of the people in the room feel the same way. It takes practice, but most importantly, you will be good at it in no time.

Look for someone who may be alone and probably has the same look as you. Walk up to them and say, "Hi" or "Hello, my name is James, I don't believe we've met." And the usual response is, "No we haven't, I am Jamal." Your response: "It is nice to meet you, Jamal."

You can ask if they are there alone, if they know the host, if it is their first time being there, and the conversation may continue by their answers. If the person really seems disinterested, don't force it. Tell them it was nice meeting them and you hope they will enjoy themselves.

At some point you may see the person again while you are speaking to someone else and you can introduce them to your new acquaintance. Start with the person you are currently speaking to and say, "John, I want you to meet Jamal, we met earlier tonight; Jamal, this is John."

When doing introductions, you are going to introduce an older adult first to a younger person, then the younger person to the older adult. The host of the party should be introduced first to any guest. Usually you introduce the lesser-known person to the more important person first, then the more known person to the lesser-known person—for example, introduce your new friend to your best friend, then your best friend to your new friend.

SALUTATION ETIQUETTE EXERCISE

1. Always waiting for someone to introduce themselves to you first is polite.

   True or False

2. When your old friend approaches you after you meet someone new you should:

   a) excuse yourself from the new friend and go hang out with your old friend.

   b) don't introduce your new friend unless your old friend asks who they are.

   c) hold separate conversations so your old friend won't feel jealous.

   d) introduce your new friend first to your old friend.

   e) tell your old friend you will catch up later and stay with your new friend.

SPORTS AND ETIQUETTE

In this time and age, we are all in for sports. Everyone wants to be the best, win it all and be champions. There are lessons to be learned in any sport. Everyone strives to be excellent, to never give up and compete until the end. You must be graceful at winning just as well as when you lose. In winning you don't want to gloat or boast about it, regardless of how the other team was acting beforehand. It is better to share the joy with all of your teammates for contributing to the win.

You also want to congratulate the other team for a hard-fought game. You don't want to celebrate in front of the other team. Wait until you have your private time in the locker room or a private place to meet. If you should lose, congratulate the other team for a game well played. Don't blame your own teammates for the loss but focus on what went wrong and how you are going to play better the next game.

If you are a spectator, there should be no taunting of the other team or referees. You want to cheer for your team without ridiculing the other team. If your team should win, don't shade the other team for the loss; cheer them on for a game well played. If you lose, don't be upset with your team for the loss but cheer them on for playing a good game. Do not yell bad things at the referees or other spectators.

SPORTS AND ETIQUETTE EXERCISE

1. To be the best, you have to show the other team in the end who is the best.

   True or False

2. It is better to show the other team why you won so it will be easier the next time you play them.

   True or False

3. If you are the best player on the team, you have to take charge and rule everyone to keep from losing.

   True or False

HUMBLE ETIQUETTE

As young men, we hear that it is all about winning, being right, being the best, crushing the competition! That's the wrong message we give to young men because it can become too toxic, and that masculinity makes it hard to make friendships and build relationships.

Humility is being able to step back and let someone else have the stage, letting them have their moment to shine. As Black boys, you are always fighting to have respect and honor that sometimes isn't given to you but you still must be humble enough to share those moments with others.

It is great to acknowledge someone else's accolades and success; that's showing humility and having good manners! As young men you are so often told to be a man and stand up, show some guts, be strong, be the winner. It is better to acknowledge your friends when they have success and support them.

Being a braggart all of the time and wielding that power around will get you nowhere! It can lead to other problems such as not having a good relationship with your partner. Having good etiquette (knowing the rules) does not mean showing off what you have and know, but means being respectful and courteous to others.

How you treat others can go a long way. It makes everyone around you better and more comfortable. Use words that will make someone feel better, not worse. This can be hard but practice makes perfect. How you treat someone can really make their day. How you use your words can go a long way in being mannerable, and others might follow your lead.

HUMBLE ETIQUETTE EXERCISE

1. You cannot show weakness when you lose in a competition; stand tall.

   True or False

2. Losers never win and winners never lose.

   True or False

3. You shouldn't let the winners know they are good because it will be harder to play them next time.

   True or False

ETIQUETTE AND BULLYING

Bullying is the most common form of social violence among youth. You have to stand up for the weaker kid. You have to stop being mean to others. It is all about power and control. You can set an example for others by refusing to participate in such acts and not just stand by and do nothing. If you do, then you are helping the perpetrators.

Be a friend to that person—it is not only good manners but it shows you have some class about yourself. You may be excluded from popular groups because you stood up for kids being bullied. This is about humanity and having good manners. There are three types of bullying: physical, emotional and cyber.

As I stated in the Social Media section, once you have said something online or on the internet you cannot take it back—it is out there. No matter how much YOU delete your posts, other people might have screenshots of what you said or did and can repost your actions at any time.

Families and schools have been sued because of the harm bullying or sexual harassment has caused. Forcing someone to do something they don't wish to do, whether it is sexual in nature or simply to have power over another person, is wrong!

You cannot force someone to have sex just because YOU want it and they are not ready. This comes from the toxic nature of patriarchy, a system of society or government where men hold the power and women are excluded from it. This type of culture is toxic and unaccepted in our society today. If she said NO or YOU said NO, it needs to be listened to and followed.

As I previously stated, sexual harassment and bullying is all about power and control. Constantly asking someone to have sex or touching their bodies when they have repeatedly told you no or stop doesn't mean that you can continue. Do not assume they are just playing hard-to-get. Even if you hear they are playing hard-to-get because they like you and they just want the attention, you still have to respect their wishes.

Girls can also harass and pressure boys to have sex. If you are not ready, then they should respect your wishes. There's a lot of pressure that comes with having sex, which we'll get into at a later chapter.

A lot of people also look at these instances as "boys being boys" or "they were just committing a prank." Well, these pranks can harm people mentally as well as physically. If you see these acts taking place, you must speak up about it to someone. Escort that person to a safe area where they can gather themselves to move on; THAT'S being the gentleman that you are looking to be. Make sure to tell an adult so they can get further help.

It may come as a shock, but it all can start from someone making a comment about a girl's tight-fitting jeans. Some young people feel it is okay to comment on girls' attire because that's what they want you to do. To sexualize anybody's image is not the way to go about making comments. Imagine if those statements were always being directed at your family member—I am sure you would want that person to stop. It takes men to stop the harassing and bullying. Men perpetuate it more often and it is passed on from one generation to another.

This patriarchal society supports it because it is our culture where men rule and women have to accept the consequences without justice. Even in this twenty-first century, women are still fighting for equal rights. When the deck is stacked against you it is hard to be heard, let alone believed.

When no one intervenes or says anything while unwelcome and inappropriate sexual remarks or physical advances are being made, it is called sexual harassment. A lot of times sexual harassment isn't taken seriously by onlookers or authorities: when there isn't any physical proof that someone was touched, the victim didn't yell or scream, it can be interpreted as being justified or the accusations were not true.

We are conditioned by the media that sex is okay and all men are alluring and are to be satisfied by women. Treating women poorly and casting disparaging remarks about people of color is just wrong. In commercials, on billboards or in the news, Black boys are represented as dangerous and monstrous. Assuming all members of the Black race act a particular way is called stereotyping. We are conditioned to think that way and it is assumed that's how we act. *No*, that's not how we act. We are descendants of Kings and Queens from the continent of Africa. Our royalty must be displayed by your actions, grace and humility. If society doesn't respect our history, then surely you must.

You don't have to be that stereotype they display of us. You are not going to be a statistic and be left fallen by the wayside. You are beautiful and intelligent and you will treat others in a respectable way.

ETIQUETTE AND BULLYING EXERCISE

1. Bullying is about:

    a) getting even

    b) power and control

    c) who's the strongest

    d) who's more popular

2. If a person is being bullied you should:

    a) watch but make sure it is evenly matched

    b) don't tell because it will make them tougher

    c) make them fight back so they won't get bullied again

    d) step in and stop it

3. There are three types of bullying:

    a) physical, emotional and financial

    b) physical, financial and hypocritical

    c) physical, emotional and cyber

    d) emotional, financial and cyber

4. Our patriarchal society supports:

    a) all humans as equals

    b) men first for their needs

    c) women first, then children

    d) only women

5. Sexual harassment is about:

    a) power and control

    b) men having their desires met

    c) women pretending they don't want to be bothered

    d) none of the above

6. If a girl says no to sex, she really wants you to pursue her more:

    True or False

7. Women or girls who wear alluring clothing really want you to comment about their shape and how they look:

    True or False

ETIQUETTE AND LGBTQ

When others respect you for who and what you are, it should be the highest compliment that you can receive. So why is it any different if someone wants to love the same sex? We are a tolerant people and an understanding people. We understand what it means to be shut out and not accepted. This is a new day and age where the youth of today have dropped a lot of the biases that have carried over the years. It is time that you do the same and accept people for who they are.

Sometimes pressure comes from some of our family members who cannot accept it, but you don't have to be pulled into that thinking. So often we may be told that they choose to be that way. They could change if they would just stop wearing those types of clothes. If they prayed more, they could change. That's not true at all. Those feelings that are inside of them cannot be changed by the wave of a hand.

Some teens are experimenting with their feelings and just want to know where they are in life, and maybe you are too. So what do you do? Give time, space and acceptance. If you are not sure about your feelings, then certainly find someone who you can trust to talk to, someone who has information and guidance for you.

ETIQUETTE AND LGBTQ EXERCISE

1. Some things have changed for today's youth:

    a) dropped biases

    b) stayed out of the fray

    c) kept fewer friends

    d) none of the above

2. To keep from being LGBTQ, one should:

    a) pray more

    b) stop wearing other gender's clothing

    c) be with more straight friends

    d) accept their choice and support it

    e) none of the above

3. Teens who are LGBTQ are:

    a) sometimes experimenting with their feelings

    b) were born with those feelings

    c) brave in declaring their choices

    d) all of the above

ETIQUETTE AND BODY IMAGE

While in your teen years, you may feel that you have to fit in to be with the popular group of friends and pop culture. Usually we will try to dress according to the group we hang out with. Maybe all of your friends wear "hoodies," sneakers and jeans. Some of you may be with the arts crowd wearing loud colors, dyed hair and fashionable clothing. All in all, the aim of our choice of style and fashion is to get the focus off of our bodies and into that in which we are invested.

In dealing with your body image, know that it is going to change as you get older. You can take care of your body now by eating right, exercising and getting proper rest. To shame someone for their body image is totally unacceptable and NOT good manners. Similar to bullying, teasing someone about their body is not in the best interest of keeping good friends.

We must respect each other and celebrate our differences. Some of you will have problems with getting your weight down, curing your acne or navigating a disability that you cannot control. Making fun of or shunning individuals who are different from you doesn't put you in the light of being a good leader.

On the other hand, most teens with disabilities want to be normal just like the rest of their classmates. They may not want to be over-nurtured, as if they are incapable of handling things themselves. It is okay to ask if they wish to talk about their disability and how they see themselves with everyone else. Maybe they don't want help all of the time; maybe they want to figure things out for themselves. Communicating with someone is the best way to know how they feel.

Getting to know your body is something you will have to understand culturally because we generally accept ourselves the way we are. We have all shapes and sizes in our community and have a lot of people who are confident in who they are. You will see women who are very hippy in the legs and buttocks and are proud of who they are. And there are women who are thin and tall and believe they are fine with themselves also. Teasing them for what they are not isn't something you should do.

The Manners Playbook

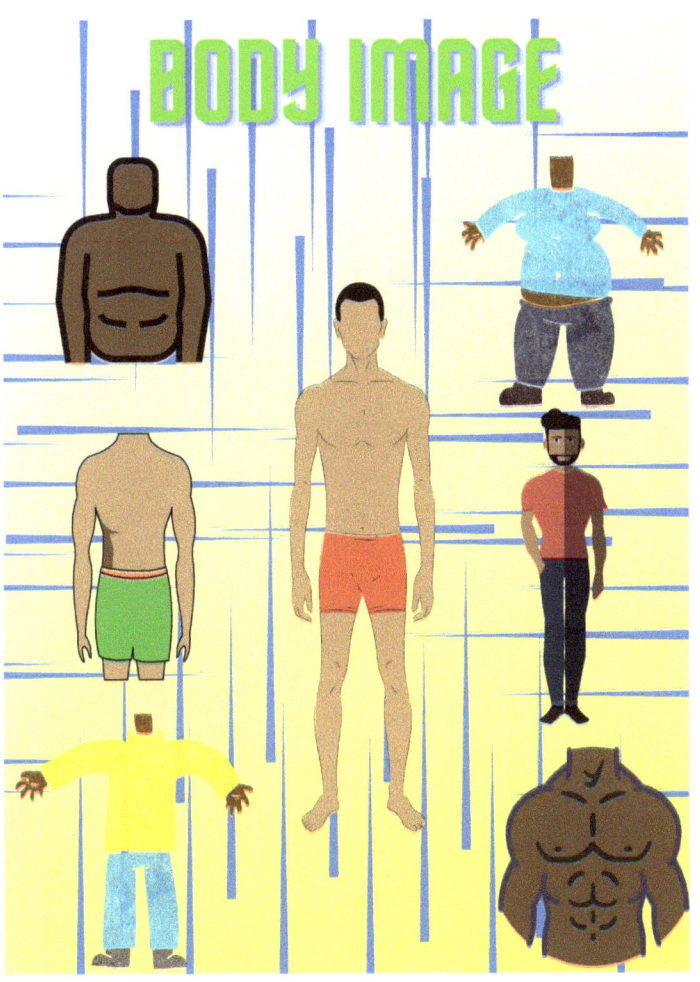

This also goes for the guys who are still short and small in stature but feel good where they are growing with their bodies. Like I said earlier, most bodies will change as you get older, and depending on how you take care of yourself, your body may change a lot.

ETIQUETTE AND BODY IMAGE EXERCISE

1. Women who are very hippy and have well-defined buttocks usually want to lose weight.

   True or False

2. It is best to tell your friends how they look so they won't get embarrassed.

   True or False

SEX AND ETIQUETTE

Making the decision to have sex carries a lot of stress on a person your age. Sometimes the pressure of not having the experience of having sex can force you to make the wrong decision. It is okay to say you are not ready.

Are you and your partner ready to date or do you just have a crush on each other? Can you face the person the next day if it doesn't turn out right? What do you want to do moving forward, continue your relationship or move on? Will your partner accept those decisions? What are their feelings about it? Will it destroy the relationship you now have with your partner?

There are so many things that can go wrong if you are having sex at an early age or if you are not ready. For instance, will she get pregnant? Will either one of you get an STD?

Having sex is a personal choice you will have to make and live with forever. If you are under the age of eighteen, I would suggest you wait. There's no rush in taking that pressure on, regardless how many of your friends are egging you on. You will know when the time is right and it will definitely be when you are older.

SEX AND ETIQUETTE EXERCISE

1. Teen couples (boyfriends and girlfriends) have more fun than singles.

   True or False

2. It is best to have sex at an early age and get it over with.

   True or False

3. If your partner says "no" to sex, they really mean "yes" because they want to see if you care.

   True or False

ETIQUETTE EXERCISE ANSWERS

What Is Etiquette?

1. d

2. b

Rules of etiquette came from <u>Egypt</u>. <u>Etiquette</u> is how you behave according to the rules that you were reared with in your culture.

Etiquette is <u>little signs</u> that can guide you along the way to being <u>hospitable.</u>

The Instructions of Ptahhotep was written to <u>teach youth how to live</u>.

Public Etiquette

1. F
2. T

3. T

4. T

5. F

Neighborly Etiquette

1. Help with trash cans.

2. Shovel snow for the elderly.

3. Don't walk/cut across their lawn.

(There are many more.)

Health Etiquette

1. drink more water, exercise more, cut down on junk food, cut down on fried foods

2. F

3. F

4. F

Dressing with Etiquette

1. F
2. F
3. c

Home Etiquette

1. F
2. F
3. F
4. F

Table Etiquette

1. c
2. a
3. b
4. a
5. right

6. F

7. F

8. c

9. F

Restaurant Etiquette

1. F

2. F

3. F

4. F

5. c

Conversation Etiquette

1. F

2. b

Guest Etiquette

1. b
2. F
3. F
4. F

Friendship Etiquette

1. c
2. F
3. T
4. F
5. T
6. F
7. T

Social Media Etiquette

1. F
2. F
3. F
4. F
5. F

Teacher Etiquette

1. F
2. F

Travel Etiquette

1. b
2. d
3. F
4. F

Adults and Etiquette

1. F
2. b
3. F
4. F
5. F

Etiquette and Gratitude

1. F

Salutation Etiquette

1. F
2. d

Sports and Etiquette

1. F
2. F
3. F

Humble Etiquette

1. T
2. F
3. F

Etiquette and Bullying

1. b
2. d
3. c
4. b
5. a
6. F
7. F

Etiquette and LGBTQ

1. a
2. d
3. d

Etiquette and Body Image

1. F

2. F

Sex and Etiquette

1. F

2. F

3. F

REFERENCES

How Rude! The Teenagers' Guide to Good Manners, Proper Behavior, and Not Grossing People Out by Alex J. Packer

Letitia Baldrige's New Manners for New Times by Letitia Baldrige

Teen Manners: From Malls to Meals to Messaging by Cindy Senning and Peggy Post

Style Over Substance by Ron Mills and Allen Huff

Notoriously Dapper by Kelvin Davis

Essential Manners for Men by Peter Post

The Guide to Good Manners for Kids by Cindy Senning and Peggy Post

Emily Post's Etiquette by Emily Post

Black Child Journal(s) by Paul Hill

NOTES

NOTES

NOTES

ABOUT THE AUTHOR

James B. Wingo has dedicated much of his life to helping young people. In New York, Mr. Wingo was a counselor for the Boys Choir of Harlem and a school counselor, assistant principal, and supervisor of counseling in the New York Public School system. He was executive director for the Cleveland Municipal School District, overseeing Student and Family Support Services.

A Cleveland native, Wingo graduated from Cleveland State University with a bachelor's degree in urban studies and business management. He holds two master's degrees from Brooklyn College in guidance and counseling and supervision and administration. Mr. Wingo is the president/founder of GLOBAL Educational Consulting Services. He is an NPCL Certified Trainer, a member of The Healthy Fathering Collaborative of Cleveland, Ohio, and a participant in Cuyahoga County's Fatherhood Initiative.

Wingo counts being a father as one of his greatest accomplishments. When he isn't helping others, he loves to travel and spend time with his family.

> Learn more at globalecs.net and
> on Instagram @globalecs

CREATING DISTINCTIVE BOOKS WITH INTENTIONAL RESULTS

We're a collaborative group of creative masterminds with a mission to produce high-quality books to position you for monumental success in the marketplace.

Our professional team of writers, editors, designers, and marketing strategists work closely together to ensure that every detail of your book is a clear representation of the message in your writing.

Want to know more?
Write to us at info@publishyourgift.com
or call (888) 949-6228

Discover great books, exclusive offers, and more at
www.PublishYourGift.com

Connect with us on social media

@publishyourgift

www.ingramcontent.com/pod-product-compliance
Lightning Source LLC
Chambersburg PA
CBHW061728070526
44583CB00024B/3055